EDGE BOOKS

MAGIC TRICKS

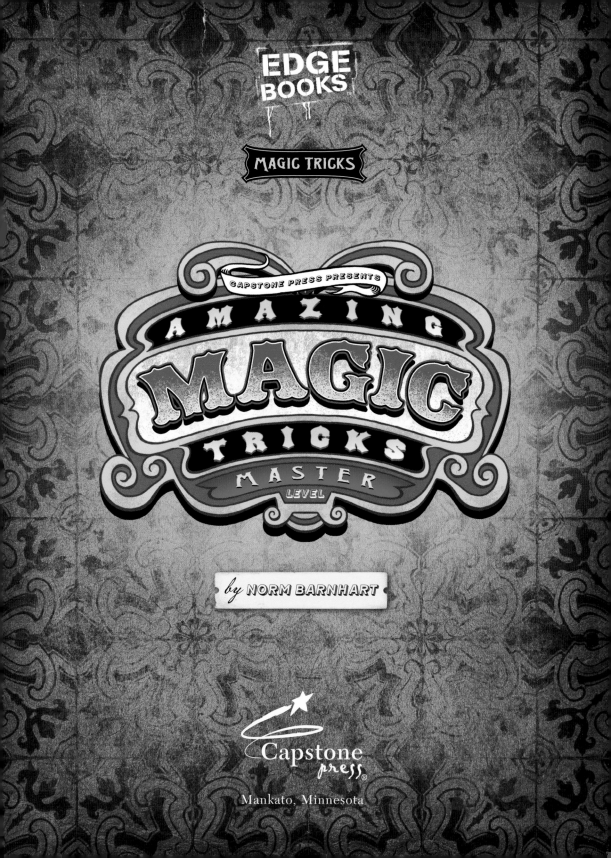

CAPSTONE PRESS PRESENTS

AMAZING
MAGIC
TRICKS
MASTER
LEVEL

by NORM BARNHART

Capstone
press

Mankato, Minnesota

Edge Books are published by Capstone Press,
151 Good Counsel Drive, P.O. Box 669, Mankato, Minnesota 56002.
www.capstonepress.com

Library of Congress Cataloging-in-Publication Data
Barnhart, Norm.
    Amazing magic tricks: master level / by Norm Barnhart.
    p. cm. — (Edge books. Magic Tricks.)
    Includes bibliographical references and index.
    Summary: "Step-by-step instructions and clear photos describe how to
perform magic tricks at the master level" — Provided by publisher.
    ISBN-13: 978-1-4296-1944-8 (hardcover)
    ISBN-10: 1-4296-1944-9 (hardcover)
    1. Magic tricks — Juvenile literature. I. Title. II. Series.
GV1548.B36 2009
793.8 — dc22   2008002575

Editorial Credits
Aaron Sautter, editor; Bob Lentz, designer/illustrator; Marcy Morin, scheduler

Photo Credits
Capstone Press/Karon Dubke, cover, objects, magic steps
Shutterstock, 9 (desert scene); Chen Ping Hung; javarman; Marilyn Volan;
    Tatiana53; Tischenko Irina, backgrounds

Capstone Press thanks Anthony Wacholtz of Compass Point Books and
Hilary Wacholz of Picture Window Books for their help in producing this book.

1 2 3 4 5 6 13 12 11 10 09 08

TABLE OF CONTENTS

BOOK
4

FANTASTIC MAGIC!

Welcome to the world of magic! With this book you'll learn some of the secrets behind magicians' amazing tricks. But magicians aren't just tricksters. They also work hard to entertain their audiences. Whether you plan to perform for a few friends or a large crowd, your main job is to make sure your audience enjoys the show. Now let's learn how to do some fantastic magic!

THE KEYS TO MAGIC

→ Practice, practice, practice! If you want your tricks to work right, you need to practice until you can do them quickly and smoothly. Try standing in front of a mirror while practicing. Then you can see what the tricks will look like to your audience.

→ Keep it secret! Magicians never share their secrets. If you reveal the secrets of a trick, people won't be very impressed. It also ruins the trick for other magicians who want to do it in the future.

→ Be entertaining! Try telling the audience some jokes or stories that relate to your tricks while performing them. Keep the audience entertained and they won't notice how the tricks are done. It will also keep them coming back for more.

MISDIRECTION

Most magicians hide their props in a magic box. A magic box will help you keep your tricks organized and your special props hidden from the audience. You can make your own magic box. Find a cardboard box and decorate it with some colorful stars, or cover it with dark cloth so it looks mysterious.

A magic wand is one of a magician's most useful tools. Wands help direct people's attention to what you want them to see. You can make a wand out of a wooden dowel painted black and white. Or roll up a piece of black construction paper and tape the ends. You can add sparkles and stars if you wish. Be creative and have fun!

A MAGIC SECRET - MISDIRECTION

Misdirection is an important part of magic. People tend to follow a magician's gaze to whatever he or she looks at. Magicians misdirect audiences by focusing their eyes on what they want people to see. Then they can secretly hide an object while the audience's attention is on something else. With enough practice, you can become a master of misdirection too!

THE IMPOSSIBLE COIN

Magicians have been doing coin tricks for thousands of years. This trick will really stump your audience. People won't believe their eyes when a coin disappears into thin air!

WHAT YOU NEED:

→ One playing card
→ Two identical coins
→ Glue

PREPARATION:

1. First, glue one coin to the face side of the playing card as shown. Then put the other coin into your pocket.

PERFORMANCE:

2. Begin by telling the audience how tricky money can be. Say, "Sometimes coins disappear right out of my hand!" Then show them the card with the coin. Be sure not to tip it, or they will see that the coin is stuck to the card.

3. Next, turn the card toward you as shown and pretend to dump the coin into your hand. Turning the card toward you keeps people from seeing that the coin is stuck to the card.

4. Now close your hand and pretend to hold the coin. Then toss the card into your magic box and pick up your magic wand.

5. Tap your hand with the wand three times. Then open your hand to show the coin has vanished.

6. Finally, reach into your pocket and bring out the second coin. The audience will believe it's the same coin that just vanished. They'll really wonder how the coin jumped from your hand into your pocket!

THE TRICKY LIZARD

Most reptiles aren't very fast. But this tricky lizard can zip out of sight in a split second. Your audience will have a good laugh when they see it climbing on your back!

WHAT YOU NEED:

- → A large piece of cardboard
- → A small toy lizard
- → Black thread
- → A safety pin
- → A black shirt or jacket

1

Pin

PREPARATION:

1. First, draw a desert scene on the cardboard with lots of cactuses, sand, and tumbleweeds. Next, tie one end of the thread to the safety pin and the other end to the toy lizard. Then attach the pin to the back of your shirt or jacket collar as shown.

2. Next, bring the toy lizard under your arm so the thread runs under it as shown. Then place the lizard in your chest pocket. The audience should not be able to see the thread when it's hidden against the black shirt or jacket.

2

Thread

3. Pull the toy lizard out of your pocket and show it to the audience. Tell them a story about how hard it is to keep track of the tricky reptile. Let them know it often disappears and tries to get back to its desert home.

4. Next, cover the lizard with the desert picture as shown. As you do this, secretly drop the lizard and let it swing around to land on your back. Then pull away the picture to show that the lizard has vanished!

5. Now pretend to look around for the tricky lizard. Where did it go? Ask the audience if they saw where it went. Finally, turn around. The audience will see the lizard hanging on your back. Act amazed and confused about how it got there. The audience will get a big laugh out of this trick!

THE MAGIC ACE

The Ace of Spades is the world's most magical card. This trick will blow your friends away when the ace turns invisible and magically appears in your pocket!

WHAT YOU NEED:

→ Two identical Ace of Spades
→ Seven other cards, any color
→ Glue
→ Scissors
→ A table

PREPARATION:

1. First put one Ace of Spades in your pocket. Then cut the other ace in half diagonally and glue one half to another card as shown.

2. The secret to this trick is in how you hold the cards. The Ace of Spades can be seen when the cards are fanned out one way. But when the cards are turned around and fanned out again, the ace is hidden.

3. First, tell the audience a story about the magical ace. Say, "The Ace of Spades can turn invisible any time it wants." Next, fan the cards out so the audience can see the ace. Ask someone if they can see the Ace of Spades. Then turn the cards over and pretend to take out an invisible card as shown.

4. Next, put down the cards and pretend to put the invisible ace in your pocket. Then, pick up the cards again. As you pick them up, be sure to turn the cards around. Keep talking to the audience as you do this so they don't notice that you turn the cards around. Now fan out the cards again and show the audience that the Ace of Spades has disappeared!

5. Finally, reach into your pocket and pull out the secret Ace of Spades. Show it to your audience. Ask them to give the ace a round of applause as you pretend that it takes a bow!

TOMMY, THE TRAINED PING-PONG BALL

Normal ping-pong balls just bounce around a lot. But this magic ping-pong ball can do a great trick. People will be astonished when it does an amazing balancing act!

WHAT YOU NEED:

→ A ping-pong ball
→ A magic wand
→ Black thread
→ Tape
→ Scissors

PREPARATION:

1. First, cut a piece of thread a little longer than the magic wand. Then use small pieces of tape to attach the thread to the wand on both ends. Make sure the thread stays a little loose in the middle.

PERFORMANCE:

2. Start by bouncing the ping-pong ball on the table a couple of times. Tell the audience a story about the ball. Say, "Tommy looks like a normal ping-pong ball. But he is really a magic ball. He can do a fun balancing act!"

3. When you're ready to do the trick, hold the wand with your thumbs under the thread as shown. The thread will help balance the ball.

4. Be sure to keep the thread facing you so the audience can't see it. Now place the ball on the wand and balance it on the thread.

5. To the audience, the ball will look like it is balancing on the wand. Gently tilt the wand up and down a little so the ball travels back and forth. The ball will seem to be doing a dangerous balancing act.

To end the trick, toss the ball up in the air, catch it, and toss it to someone in the audience. While they look at it, toss the wand into your magic box. Then ask the audience for a round of applause for the tricky ball!

THE NUMBER ONE FAN

This trick will astound any sports fan. Your audience will be stunned when you pull a big league sports star out of a hat!

WHAT YOU NEED:

+ A giant foam finger
+ A baseball hat
+ 2 identical sports cards
+ 5 other sports cards
+ Tape

PREPARATION:

1. First, place a circle of tape on the back of one of the identical cards. Then tuck the secret card into the baseball hat along one side as shown. Be sure the tape faces the inside of the hat and isn't stuck on anything.

PERFORMANCE:

2. Begin by asking if there are any sports fans in the audience. Then bring out the cards and name off the players. Lay the cards on the table as shown. Make sure the second identical card is the third card in from your left. Next, ask someone to choose a number between one and six.

Forced card

If they say, "One," start at your left and spell out O, N, E as shown.

If they say, "Two," start at your left and spell out T, W, O as shown.

If they say, "Three," start at your left and count 1, 2, 3 as shown.

If they say, "Four," start from your right and count 1, 2, 3, 4 as shown.

If they say, "Five," start at your right again and spell out F, I, V, E as shown.

If they say, "Six," start at your left and spell S, I, X as shown.

TURN PAGE FOR MORE!

Secret card

3. When you land on the forced card, hold it up and tell the audience which one it is. Now show them your magic foam finger. Say, "This magic finger can help me find the chosen card." Next, hold up the hat to show that it's empty. Be sure to cover the secret card with your hand as shown so the audience can't see it.

4. Now toss all the cards into the hat and shake them up a little. Don't shake too hard or the secret card might fall in with the rest of the cards. The rest of the trick will be ruined if this happens.

magic tip: When you count out the cards based on a chosen number, you will always land on the card you want. This is called "forcing" a card.

5. Next, put on the magic foam finger and dip it into the hat as shown. Make it fun for the audience by pretending to dig around inside the hat a little. You can even pretend that the finger gets stuck on something. When you're ready for the big finish, press the finger against the tape on the secret card so it sticks to the end.

6. Finally, slowly pull the foam finger out of the hat. Show the audience that the chosen card is magically stuck on the end. Say, "The magic finger never fails to find the card!" Then take a bow as the audience applauds!

THE COIN MULTIPLYING BOOK

Sometimes coins are found in the strangest places. This trick will stun your audience when a magic book instantly multiplies the coins in a volunteer's hands.

WHAT YOU NEED:

→ Eight coins
→ An old book
→ Scissors
→ Glue

PREPARATION:

1. First, make a secret pocket in the old book. Cut out a small space at the bottom of the book as shown. Make sure the pocket is big enough to fit two coins inside. Don't make it too big or the audience might see the hole.

2. Next, glue the pages together around the secret pocket as shown. When the glue is dry, place two coins in the secret pocket.

3. Tell the audience about your special magic book. Say, "This magic book can instantly make coins multiply." Then place six coins on top of the book. Ask a volunteer to help you with this trick. Ask the volunteer to count the coins out loud. Then quickly tip the book so all the coins, including the hidden ones, slide into the volunteer's hand.

4. Tell the volunteer to hold the coins tightly in his or her hand. Then lightly tap the book two times on top of the volunteer's hand. Ask, "Did you feel anything happen inside your hand?" The volunteer will probably say they didn't feel anything at all.

5. Finally, ask the volunteer to put the coins on the table and count them out loud again. The audience will be amazed when they see there are now eight coins. Thank the volunteer and ask the audience to give him or her a round of applause!

magic tip: Always keep the secret pocket facing you so the audience and volunteer can't see the hole with the hidden coins.

THE SPOOKY SPOON

Even ghosts like going on picnics. Your friends will be spooked when this ghostly spoon disappears right before their eyes! With practice, you can make this simple trick look awesome!

WHAT YOU NEED:

- A plastic spoon
- About 2 feet (0.6 meter) of thin elastic
- A safety pin
- A jacket with long sleeves
- An electric drill

PREPARATION:

1. First, ask an adult to drill a small hole in the end of the spoon handle as shown. Then tie one end of the elastic through the hole in the spoon and the other end to the safety pin.

2. Next, connect the safety pin to the inside of your jacket at the shoulder. Then run the spoon and elastic down the inside of the jacket sleeve as shown.

3. Just before you do this trick, step off the stage or behind the curtain so the audience can't see you. Pull the spoon out of your sleeve and hold it in your hand as shown. Then tell the audience a story about the ghostly spoon. Say, "This spooky spoon belongs to a ghost. Sometimes it takes the spoon back without any warning!"

4. Now cover the spoon with both hands. Begin rubbing your hands together in a mysterious way.

5. When you cover the spoon, let it go so the elastic can pull it back up your sleeve as shown.

6. Finally, open your hands and show the audience that the spoon has vanished into thin air. Say, "I guess the ghost was ready for his dinner and wanted his spoon back!"

THE MAGIC MATCHBOX BANK

You can save money without making a trip to the bank! Just sprinkle some magic dust and your coins travel to a safe place. This magical traveling penny will keep your audience in awe.

WHAT YOU NEED:

→ Two pennies with the same date
→ An empty matchbox

PREPARATION:

1. Place one of the pennies between the inner and outer parts of the matchbox as shown. Make sure the penny is completely covered so the audience won't see it.

PERFORMANCE:

2. First, show the audience that the matchbox is empty. Say, "I've found a new kind of savings bank." Then close the box so the secret penny slides into it, and set it aside. Next, take out the second penny and ask a volunteer to read the date.

3. Take back the penny and hold it between your thumb and first finger. Then pretend to grab the penny with your other hand. Instead of grabbing it, you will drop it into your palm as shown. It looks like you're holding the coin in the second hand, but you are really hiding it in the palm of the first hand. This old trick is called the French Drop.

4. Now reach into your pocket for some magic dust. Leave the hidden penny in your pocket, then sprinkle magic dust over your empty hand.

5. Next, open your hands wide to show the audience that the penny has vanished!

6. Finally, open the matchbox and take out the secret penny. Show it to the audience and ask the volunteer to read the date again. They will be stunned at how the penny magically traveled from your hand to the matchbox!

THE EGG-STRAORDINARY EGG

Are you ever in a hurry and don't have time for lunch? With this fun trick you can make an egg magically appear and cook it up fast. You'll leave the audience wondering how it's done!

WHAT YOU NEED:

> A hat
> A handkerchief
> A plastic egg
> A plastic "cooked" egg
> A plate
> Thread
> A needle

PREPARATION:

1. Ask an adult to help you prepare this trick. First, poke two small holes in one end of the plastic egg with the needle. Then slide the thread through the holes and tie it to the egg as shown. Make sure the thread is the same color as your hanky.

2. Next, sew the other end of the thread to the hanky. The plastic egg should be about 1 inch (2.5 centimeters) from the edge of the hanky as shown. Finally, put the plastic "cooked" egg into the hat.

"Cooked" egg

3. First, tell the audience that you're feeling hungry. Say, "I think it's time for a snack." Then pick up the hat and show the audience that it's empty. When you pick it up, hide the "cooked" egg under your hand as shown. Then put the hat down and let the "cooked" egg drop into it.

4. Next, pick up the hanky by the corners as shown so the egg hangs behind the hanky. Be sure to do this with the egg facing you so the audience can't see it.

5. Now fold the hanky in half with the egg inside. Hold it above the hat and say, "Cluck, Cluck, Cluck!" Then let the egg fall from the hanky into the hat as shown.

6. Next, quickly drag the hanky over the hat. Then raise it up so the egg is lifted out of the hat and hidden like before. Toss the hanky and egg into your magic box. Now pick up the hat and pretend to "cook" the egg inside by blowing on it. Finally, flip the hat over the plate and show the audience your delicious cooked egg!

THE AMAZING HEALING ROPE

Your audience will have a great time with this funny rope trick. They'll think you goofed at first. But they'll be stunned when the rope is magically healed right before their eyes!

WHAT YOU NEED:

→ Two pieces of rope about 3 feet (1 meter) long
→ Two pieces of rope about 4 inches (10 centimeters) long
→ Two large paper bags
→ Scissors
→ Tape

PREPARATION:

1. First, cut one of the paper bags in half lengthwise as shown.

2. Then tape the half bag inside the whole bag to make a secret pocket as shown.

3. Next, make a small loop about 1 foot (0.3 meter) from the end of one of the long ropes. Then tie a loose knot around the loop with one of the short rope pieces as shown above. The long rope should look like it has been cut and tied back together.

4. Now tie another knot in the same way about 1 foot (0.3 meter) from the other end of the long rope. The rope should now look similar to the picture.

5. Place the knotted rope into the paper bag. Leave the secret pocket empty.

TURN PAGE FOR MORE!

6. First, tell the audience that you have a trick that will astound them. Then show them the second long rope and say, "This amazing magic rope can heal itself if it's cut." Then hold up the rope and cut it into three equal pieces.

7. Next, slide the three pieces of rope into the secret pocket in the paper bag. Don't let the audience see the secret pocket!

8. Now shake the bag around a little. Pretend that the pieces of rope are jumping around inside and are trying to heal themselves. You can also wave your magic wand over the bag as you do this.

9. Next, reach into the bag and pull out the knotted rope. Toss the bag out of sight. Say, "The rope is whole again! Isn't that amazing?" The audience will probably laugh when they see that the rope is just tied together. Try acting confused. But tell them that you can fix it. You just need a volunteer's help. Ask someone to help you fix the rope.

10. Ask the volunteer to blow on one of the knots. As he or she blows, pull the rope tight as shown. The knot should pop right off the rope. Say, "Wow! You're better at this than I thought!"

11. Finally, ask the volunteer to blow on the other knot. Pull the rope tight so the other knot pops off like before. Show the magically healed rope to the audience. Thank the volunteer and ask him or her to take a bow while the audience gives you both a round of applause!

GLOSSARY

applause (uh-PLAWZ) — clapping hands to show appreciation or approval

audience (AW-dee-uhns) — people who watch or listen to a play, movie, or show

force card (FORSS KARD) — a card that a magician tricks an audience into choosing

French Drop (FRENCH DROP) — an old method of secretly hiding a coin in the palm of the hand to make it seem that the coin has disappeared

identical (eye-DEN-ti-kuhl) — exactly alike

misdirection (mis-di-REK-shuhn) — a method of getting an audience to look the wrong way while the magician secretly does something else

prop (PROP) — an item used by an actor or performer during a show

volunteer (vol-uhn-TIHR) — someone who offers to help perform a task during a show

READ MORE

Burgess, Ron. *Kids Make Magic! The Complete Guide to Becoming an Amazing Magician.* Charlotte, Vt.: Williamson, 2004.

Longe, Bob. *Mind-Blowing Magic Tricks.* New York: Sterling, 2007.

Zenon, Paul. *Magic of the Mind: Tricks for the Master Magician.* Amazing Magic. New York: Rosen, 2008.

INTERNET SITES

FactHound offers a safe, fun way to find Internet sites related to this book. All of the sites on FactHound have been researched by our staff.

Here's how:
1. Visit *www.facthound.com*
2. Choose your grade level.
3. Type in this book ID **1429619449** for age-appropriate sites. You may also browse subjects by clicking on letters, or by clicking on pictures and words.
4. Click on the **Fetch It** button.

FactHound will fetch the best sites for you!

About the author

Norm Barnhart is a professional comic magician who has entertained audiences for more than 28 years. In 2007, Norm was named America's Funniest Magician by the Family Entertainers Workshop. Norm's travels have taken him across the United States and to five other countries. He also loves getting kids excited about reading. Norm says, "I love bringing smiles to people's faces with magic. After reading this book, kids will love doing magic too."